Eva's Pitcher and the Panther

by Andy Bozeman

eISBN 978-1-887892-05-6

Eva's Pitcher and the Panther

Andy Bozeman

Eva's Pitcher and the Panther

My grandmother had something I really wanted. I said, "Mamaw, can I have that when you die?" "I suppose that'll be alright," she answered. "Great!" I blurted, then anxiously added, "When will that be?"

The thing I wanted was an old pitcher. It sat in a cupboard on a high shelf, and far back enough on that shelf to imply that it had been put away forever. But, on some evenings my grandmother would get it down from the shelf, rinse it out, fill it with cream, and slide it into the refrigerator to chill.

When morning came, the first rays of sunshine would find me already in my place at the table, where I would be the only one eating. Even way back in those days, personal schedules dictated that on most mornings each family member ate breakfast solo.

My father was half insurance salesman and half Methodist Minister. The pay for a minister was dismally low, so he sold life insurance to earn the money to put the cream in the pitcher. He always wore a suit and tie, and even though the tie was clip-on, making it quick to add as a finishing touch, the rest of his dressing ritual took long enough that his arrival at the breakfast table was always a distant second to mine.

My mother was the perfect wife for a minister. She was a natural helper. She had a doctor-like ability to care for anyone who was sick, a minister-like knack to console anyone who was sad, and a heart that made her want to care for everybody; and that was a good thing, because it seemed like *everybody* was either sick or sad. Her days were filled with visits to the bedsides of those who were sick in homes and hospitals, and long sessions comforting those who were sad in private parlors and prisons. She wore her Sunday-best every day, so her dressing routine, detailed and extended, resulted in third place for breakfast.

My only sibling was one sister…..she was the clever one, the pretty one, the smart one, the one most respected, most artistic, most popular, most 'likely.' Add honor roll student and head cheerleader, and it's easy to see that, as a sister, hers was a force to be reckoned with - but not at the breakfast table. Her fourth-place finish for breakfast was usually a rush-by-and-grab for a piece of toast, then out the door to some event like a football game, or cheerleader practice, or whatever meetings were attended by straight-A students. I never did know.

Eva's Pitcher and the Panther
Andy Bozeman

At the time of my grandfather's death in 1964, my mother, father, sister, and I were living in a small house across the street from the huge house that had been my grandparent's home for decades. My grandmother didn't want to live alone, and it was logical for us to move in with her. That's how it came to be that a certain pitcher was used to hold the cream that completed my bowl of cereal.

Like my mother, Mamaw was a helper, too. I was eleven and could certainly handle it myself, but she enjoyed helping me with my morning meal. It was a ritual we both enjoyed. She liked for me to just sit still. First, we would say a prayer, usually, "Heavenly Father, accept our thanks for this food and all our many other blessings. Amen." She would tilt the cereal box until its rice-shaped puffs tumbled into the bowl. Next, she would add one heaping scoop of crystals from the sugar bowl and slowly sprinkle an even layer over the cereal. Then the finale. She tilted the pitcher over the cereal until a mere trickle was pouring out. Starting at the center and tracing an outward spiral, cream slowly drizzled over the puffs. We each leaned an ear toward the bowl to listen, hoping to hear that famous snapping and crackling and popping sound that only puffed rice can make. We were never disappointed. It was my favorite breakfast moment, ever.

It was such a favorite moment, that I wanted to make sure I could live it over and over, whenever I wanted. But to do that, I had to possess the key component. That's why I asked for the pitcher.

"So, Andy, why do you want it?" Mamaw asked.

I was in the middle of relishing a full mouth of cream and sugar and puffed rice, so her question caught me off-guard. I mumbled, "Why do I want what?"

"The pitcher," she answered, "You just asked me for the pitcher. Why do you want it?"

I felt like I should have an answer less self-serving than 'It makes my cereal taste better,' so I meekly offered, "It's just special."

"You have no idea how special," she said with eyes brightening. "Have you ever looked at it real close?"

I never had. All I knew, after seeing it almost every week for two years, was that its short squat body was pale gray with a wisp of pale blue around the rim; that it had a handle that perfectly fit my young grasp; that its broad, round mouth was formed up and pinched in to make the spout; and that it kept its contents really cold. I just answered flatly, "No Ma'am, I've never looked at it real close."

"Let me show you," and she began a very eye-opening pottery tour.

The wide mouth, round at the handle, was stretched and tapered to make the spout, almost mimicking the shape of a coal scuttle. Just below the mouth, still in the pale blue, the neck of the pitcher was covered with raised-relief details. Two parallel lines about an inch apart ran all the way around. Between the lines was a series of wave-like swirls, undulating and filling the entire circumference. Under these two lines the color began to fade from blue to gray. Centered on each side was a combination of shapes that hung like a curtain beneath the two blue lines. Half a sunburst, lined within by tiny droplets, was flanked by two swirling, paisley-shaped teardrops. The tails of the tears curved in opposite directions with two meeting to make a platform for the handle, and two meeting to create a simple bracket, having the appearance of support for the spout.

"What do you think, so far?" she asked.

I wanted to sound interested but wasn't impressed. While I found these newly revealed details to be kind of attractive, in an overly simple way, I also saw that the overall quality was a mess. The glazing was poorly done. There were runs and drips in the paint. Whoever made it had left fingerprints in the clay; and under both the handle and spout it looked as though a clumsy thumb had pushed too-soft clay back into position, slashing through the raised-relief details with no apparent effort to repair the damage to the decorative designs. These newly discovered flaws diminished my desire for the pitcher. But, not wanting to disappoint my grandmother, I offered pretend approval, "It's okay, I guess."

"There's one more thing," she continued. She turned and tilted the pitcher so I could see the underside of the spout. "Right here," she pointed, "there's a big chip missing. This happened when…."

"A chip!" I interrupted. "You mean it's broken?!" That was the last straw. Runs, drips, smears, smudges, fingerprints, and now *this*? Any value it had to me instantly evaporated. "Why, it's ruined!" I judged. Then, with a full-on, totally intended, obstinate smirk I added, "Now I *don't* want it!"

Mamaw was endowed with a gracious-plenty of grandmotherly patience, which empowered her to overlook my bad attitude. "Not so fast," she cautioned. "Wait 'til you hear the story, then decide."

"There's a story?" Curiosity made my whole forehead lift up. "What story, Mamaw?"

Eva's Story :
"This ol' pitcher was a gift given to my parents on the day I was born in 1892 in Gilbertown, Alabama. It was made by a woman who was already old, before I was even thought of. Her name was Agnes. If you look on the bottom of the pitcher, near the edge, there's a tiny letter A inscribed, and near it the outline of a house. That meant 'homemade by Agnes', and everybody in the area recognized her signature. Agnes wasn't an artist and didn't claim to be. She didn't create great works for museums, things just to look at. She called herself a *maker* because everything she made was meant to *work*, just like this pitcher. It's not much to look at, but it works just fine. She made her living making things out of clay from the bottom of the Tombigbee River. She made bowls and pots and plates and candlesticks and cups for everybody. She died just a couple of years after I was born, so I'm really glad to have this.

Eva's Pitcher and the Panther
Andy Bozeman

When I was a little girl, I think I was about five years old, the spout on that pitcher got broken because me and my family, in fact our whole house, got attacked, one winter night, by a huge, wild, black panther…….and he almost got us!

My father, Papa, had bought forty acres of land from a man named Sims. Mr. Sims thought a lot of my father, so he *gave* him another forty acres. That eighty acres has been in the family for almost a hundred years.

My mother and father had married and were living with her father, Grandpa George. Their eighty acres of land was very near Grandpa George's, and so they decided to build themselves a log house about a half-a-mile from his home.

My father bought an old abandoned church made of logs and big timbers and hewn beams. He took it apart, then used mules to drag it, one log at a time, about eight miles to his land, where he put it back together to make a cabin for us to live in.

Relatives and other people came to help with the house-raisin', so it didn't take very long to build it. They built one great big room with a fireplace in it for cooking. A porch was also built around three sides of the cabin. Then, right away, they decided to fill-in one section of the porch to make a room for the children. That was my brothers and me. At that time, there were three of us children: an older brother, a younger brother, and me in the middle. Later, there was enough money from farming to build-on a real kitchen, but right then all we had was that big ol' fireplace, and we were thankful we had *it*. For the time being though, the whole house was just the 'big room' and the 'children's room'.

The cabin was almost finished, but Papa ran out of nails. The floorboards in the children's room were down, but with no nails they had to be left loose. There were also a few floorboards in the big room which weren't nailed down. Now, in those days you couldn't just run down to the neighborhood hardware store and buy a few pounds of nails. The only way to get anything was to wait for one of the big paddlewheel steam boats to come down the Tombigbee River. This river was not far from the cabin, and sometimes we got to see those big boats.

We had to move into the house before it was completely finished because it was almost spring, and the crops had to be planted. Everyone was in a hurry. All the relatives who lived nearby helped us move-in.

Papa had already built a barn, a chicken house, and some fences. He brought a rooster and some hens, a cow, and his horse and wagon. Somebody brought a cake, a homemade cake - it didn't come from a grocery store - and other good things to eat.

On this particular day, we had finished the chores and Mama - my mother - had cooked a big pot of good stew on the fireplace, made cornbread, fixed coffee for the adults, and gotten the milk from the cow. We were all tired after the day's work, but that didn't keep us from enjoying the good supper, along with cake for dessert.

As soon as it was dark, we three children went to bed in our new room, and Mama and Papa finished up the dishes and went to bed in the big room.

The first sign that this night was different was when Mama commented on how quiet it was; and she was right. Usually, even in the winter, there were night owls hooting, or whippoorwills calling, or coyotes howling. But on this moonless night there wasn't a sound. The dark woods were completely silent.

We were all sleeping soundly when we were awakened by a strange noise. It came from the woods, off in the distance, but even so, we could tell that it was very loud. It was sort of like a long, wailing cry, and at first Papa thought it might be someone yelling for help and in pain.

Papa lit a lantern. As we sat in the dim light listening, we noticed that the sound was getting closer; and Papa realized that it must be some kind of animal. He listened closely but couldn't decide what kind of animal it was. "That's not like anything I ever heard, before," he said, as he reached for the oil lantern and turned out more wick to make it brighter.

We had a great big bulldog named Bear. He was never afraid of anything. He had even pulled a man off a horse, one time. The man had ridden up on horseback with his rifle out and pointed at Papa and Bear. It was a robbery. He shouted "Gi' me all you got!", but his voice was so loud with so much snarl in it, that it set Bear off. Bear charged the horse, jumped up and grabbed the man's arm in his teeth, then pulled the man off his horse and pinned him to the ground. While the horse bolted down the road, Bear stood over the man growling, and drooling on his face, waiting for the command to kill and eat. But Papa didn't give it. Instead, Papa just took the rifle, and told the man to "Git!" The man lit out after his horse, and never came back.

That was Bear, not afraid of *anything*. So, you can imagine why we got a little concerned when Bear came scratching at the door to come in, and whimpering like a scared pup. He had never done this before, and when we let him in, he darted straight for the bed and crawled under it. This really scared us. What could it possibly be that was so terrible it scared Bear into hiding? It was then that Papa thought about the loose floorboards. If it was a dangerous animal it might be able to push up the planks and get in the house………..and get us.

My brothers and I, and our mattresses, were brought into the big room with Mama and Papa and Bear. Then, they put trunks and a table and other heavy things over all the loose floorboards in the children's room, and the big room. Finally, they closed and latched the shutters and pushed the furniture up against the outside doors. Mama's cedar hope-chest was pushed against the back door, and two chairs were piled on top. A big cupboard, still full of all our dishes, was shoved against the main door, and our big family table was pushed against it. Papa got his rifle loaded and ready and hoped that everything would hold.

By this time, the creature was coming up behind the barn. We could hear his howl as he came closer. Papa and Mama were glad they had locked the cow and horse in the barn, and the chickens in the chicken house. This had been done as part of the nightly routine so a fox couldn't get at the chickens. One thing was for sure, this was no fox. There wasn't a sound coming from inside the barn or chicken house. The farm animals were probably aware of the danger and just as scared as we were. But for all of our fear, there was nothing to be done but sit quietly and wait.

Papa was on the floor, legs crossed, his back straight against the wall, his gun ready. Bear had come out from under the bed and crawled into Papa's lap. Bear was so big it was hard to tell who was in whose lap. They looked so funny, I laughed out loud. "Shhhhh!" Papa ordered.

Papa and Mama and Bear were all squinting their eyes and concentrating hard, not so much to look *at* the walls but to listen *through* them. The creature was close now. Out there in the dark we could hear him wailing into the night and circling around the barn and the chicken house. Then the monster moved on to our cabin. It circled around the house stopping, now and then, and continually wailing that terrifying cry. We children, and Mama, huddled closer to Papa. Bear crawled under Mama's rocking chair and tried to look like he was protecting all of us, and not the other way around.

Nobody moved.

Nobody made a sound.

I don't think we even breathed.

Suddenly, we could hear scratching and crashing from the children's room. It was pushing up floorboards and lifting the furniture meant to hold them down. It was coming in!

We had Papa so surrounded he couldn't move. "Close that door!" Papa shouted to Mama. She sprang to her feet and started pushing the door to the children's bedroom shut. But she was too slow. From the other room a dark shadow charged the door and pushed back. Mama screamed – we *all* screamed – but she lowered her shoulder into that door with all her strength. She pushed back as hard as she could until the wood & leather latch caught.

The door stayed shut, but the animal on the other side tried three more times to charge the door and scratch through it. We could hear it moving around, throwing its weight against different places along the log walls. "It's trying to find a weak spot," Papa gasped, adding a whisper directed at Mama, "What *is* that?"

Then silence.

Once again, nobody moved.

Nobody made a sound. I just sat with my eyes closed, trying to listen. Where was it?

We tried not to breathe but we were out of breath from the earlier panic, so we were all panting.

Still….. there wasn't…… a sound.

My older brother muttered, "Where is it?"

Instantly a roar filled the room. The planks underneath my brother lifted up with him on top. A dark shape stabbed between the planks and into the room. It was the animal's claw trying to grab anything it could, but thankfully, it found nothing.

In the confusion the lantern was knocked over and went out. Scrambling around in the dark, we were all screaming. Bear was howling and yelping. Everyone scurried trying to find a safe place. Papa was shouting, "Where is it! I've got to shoot it!" Mama was shouting at Papa, "Don't shoot, I can't find everybody!

Screaming, yelling, howling, yelping, roaring. We ran around in the dark. We ran into walls, into furniture, into

Bear, into each other; and thinking when we ran into each other that we had run into the monster, we screamed and yelled and ran that much more. I collided with the big family table. It knocked the breath out of me, but I was still able to climb on top and stand with my back against the cupboard. That gave me a moment to calm down, so I could realize that the roaring had stopped.

I shouted, "Hey! Wait! I think it's gone!" That brought immediate calm to the others. Papa and Mama, standing together in the middle of the pitch-black room did an immediate headcount. Papa said in a hushed voice, "Eva, where are you?"

"I'm alright," I whispered. "I'm on the table."
"Good. Stay there," Papa whispered back.

Mama found each of my brothers safe in a corner. Papa found Bear hiding under the bed again.

Once again, the night was silent. "Oh, Lord," I prayed, "please let it stay this way."

Just like before, nobody moved, as if anybody any had energy left.

Everybody was breathing hard; exhausted, apprehensive, just plain scared.

I don't know how long we stayed that way. It felt like forever.

Mama whispered, "Maybe it's gone."

ROWWWRRRRRRR!!!!!!! The planks under my table lifted up, raising the table with me on it. I was thrown back hard against the cupboard. My body hit with such force it caused dishes to rain onto the floor, shattering to pieces as they hit near the darting black shape of the creature's claw jabbing into the dark for prey.

With everyone screaming, and dishes crashing and shattering, and planks and furniture clattering, and the blasted beast roaring, a turning point for Bear was reached. He'd had enough.

Bear shot from under the bed and dove across the floor, sinking his teeth into the black paw of that horrible monster. His powerful jaws clamped down and stayed tightly closed. He was not going to release his captive. The animal tried to pull back, but Bear wouldn't let go. The monster's fierce roar instantly became a shriek of pain. The sounds of clattering and upheaval of planks and furniture changed from something trying to get in to something trying to get away.

Finally, I guess Bear thought he'd made his point, and he let go. We could hear as the body of the beast bumped into beams and piers under the house as it made a hasty retreat, still shrieking in pain, until at last it was out from under the house and headed for the woods.

We all sat in silence and prayed to God for His protection and deliverance. We could tell from the sound of the wailing that the creature was headed into the woods away from us. We were so relieved but hoped that our neighbors were bolted up good and tight. "Do you think he'll go after anybody else tonight?" Mama asked. "No," Papa sighed. "I think Bear gave him enough adventure for one night."

It wasn't long before the monster was out of earshot. Even so, the farm and forest remained black as death and quiet as the grave. At last the silence was broken by the call of a far-off whippoorwill. An owl could be heard hooting as it flew across the treetops. The howl of a distant coyote joined the chorus. The night was normal. Only then did we relax enough to go back to bed. Even though we felt safer, my brothers and I still stayed in the big room the rest of the night..... Oh, and Bear?....... he stayed under the bed.

The next morning, after daylight, we went out to see if there was any damage. We found huge footprints like a cat would make but much, much larger. At the edge of the house, under the children's room, the creature had dug a hole large enough for all three of us children to get down into at the same time. This is where the monster had dug its way under the house.

In the afternoon we got word from neighbors who had heard the wailing, too. But, no one had seen what it was. It had been too dark, and they had been too afraid to go look. We were the only ones attacked.

A week later, one of the neighbors was out hunting. He was looking up toward a high hill when he saw what he believed to be a gigantic black panther crossing over the top. He shot at it but missed. They all believed *this* was the animal they had heard that night. Some people thought that it might have escaped from a circus. But if it did, it had to travel a very long way to get to our area. Fortunately, we never heard from it again."

The morning after the panther attacked, we were all working to clean up the mess. Papa was filling in the big hole outside. My brothers were putting tables and chairs back in their right place. Mama was tending to

> scattered clothes and bedding. I was picking up broken dishes and sweeping the floor. Most of the plates and cups were beyond repair, but there was one dish that survived. The clay of my cream pitcher must have been thick enough to withstand the fall to the floor. It only had one little chip missing out of the spout. Other than that, it was fine."

With her story ended she addressed me again. "So, Andy, that's the story of this cream pitcher. I hope that you'll remember that just because some things aren't perfect, it doesn't make them less valuable."

"Yes Ma'am," I grinned. "What a great story!" I was beaming. Now I *reeeealy* wanted that pitcher.

I was virtually glowing when I asked, again, "Mamaw, can I have that when you die?" Again, she answered, "I suppose that'll be alright." "Great!" I blurted. But this time I added, "It's okay if it's a long, long time."

Soon after, circumstances made it sensible for an aunt, my mother's sister, to move in with Mamaw, so we moved out. I went on with the business of my life, and as the years went by, my memory of the cream pitcher faded, to be replaced with more urgent concerns like mortgages and children.

Eva's Pitcher and the Panther

Andy Bozeman

My grandmother lived a generous number of years, but of course, ultimately her time on earth was finished. Her huge house, which was really all she had, passed into the hands of several children, brothers and sisters of my mother. The house was near a hospital that needed room to grow, so the management of the hospital made a generous offer to purchase the house from the estate. Further, because the hospital only wanted the land, the brothers and sisters were allowed to scavenge the structure for anything they wanted. As for me, I had *lived* in it. I had enjoyed it *all*. I was content just to have the memories.

Over the course of weeks that held the run-up to the tear-down, the old house was descended upon by aunts and uncles and cousins, all vying for antique furniture and fireplace mantles and claw foot tubs and vintage doors and heart pine flooring. Of course, there was also silverware and rugs and dishes.

Dishes is the keyword here, because one type of dish is a cream pitcher. It finally dawned on me that Mamaw had said I could have it.

About ten days before the end, I stopped by the old house. It was a terrible mess. Old clothes and shoes, frayed drapes, bedding and mattresses, old books and magazines, were all in a trash pile on the living room floor, along with anything and everything deemed discard-able. Fireplace mantles and doors had been hacked out of the walls, scattering gravel-sized chunks of plaster on every floor that was still in place. Floor planks had been ripped up leaving only rough pine subflooring. Plaster dust coated everything with a thick layer of gypsum snow.

All the cabinets and cupboards were completely empty. Nothing was left. The cream pitcher was gone. Someone else had it. I was disappointed, but I wasn't upset. It was my own fault. Not only was I the only person who knew about Mamaw's gift, but I had failed to collect it in a timely manner. I tried to forget about it, but the more I tried to let it go the more it haunted my thoughts. I became nostalgic remembering the times and seasons I had lived in that house and shared with Mamaw and the rest of my family. As the days passed, nostalgia turned to sadness then depression as I considered that I had failed my grandmother; that she had shared something so special with me, and I had carelessly forgotten.

I decided to go to the old house one more time. I went on a Sunday afternoon, the last day before the house would be razed. I didn't go to look for anything or to take anything. I simply went so I could stand inside that old, huge house and apologize to my grandmother; to say I was sorry I had forgotten.

There was no front door. Some cousin had removed it. I just stepped in. Since my last visit, others had left their mark with taken spoils. Plaster dust was now forming drifts in corners. No polished heart pine flooring was left; and the trash pile in the living room had grown in volume by twice.

I stood there silently, remembering the joy and peace we had all shared in that house. I started a visual scan of the trash pile, working my eyes upwards from the floor. So many things that had been thrown there as trash had been part of my existence, part of my whole extended family's existence, only a few weeks before. Halfway up, there were books that had been my grandparent's favorites. Almost to the top were tattered armchair covers that had adorned my grandfather's reading chair. But when my eyes reached the peak, I couldn't believe what I saw. On the very top of that mountain of my family-thrown-way, dust free and upright, was the cream pitcher.

I can only guess that someone had taken it in the early grab-n-go rush, then discovered the chipped spout, which of course made it worthless, then on a return trip for more worthy collectibles had tossed it away as trash.

I wasted no time performing my own grab-n-go. I snatched it from its perch and said a prayer of thanksgiving to God and to the memory of my grandmother. I left that house for the last time a proud victor and felt like my life had been restored. Ever since, I have cherished that old broken clay pot, and to this day I proudly display it in my house, where every day I can see Eva's cream pitcher and think of home.

~~~~~

Just so you know, I'm finishing this writing just before sunrise. I have a special celebration in mind. Last evening, I put cream in that old pitcher. It's been chilling in the refrigerator all night. In a minute, after I type 'The End,' I'll sit down to a bowl of cereal. I'll say my grandmother's favorite prayer for a meal, "Heavenly Father, accept my thanks for this food and all my many other blessings." But I plan to add a few words. I'll say, "Lord, thank you for log cabins and panthers, Agnes and clay from the bottom of the Tombigbee River, and Eva's cream pitcher. But mostly, thank you that my grandmother was Eva. Amen" Last and best, I will repeat my favorite breakfast moment, as the first rays of sunshine stream across the table.

THE END
~~~~~

Eva's Pitcher and the Panther

Andy Bozeman

About the Author :
Thank you for reading my story. I'm a born storyteller. When I write, it's to have fun, tumbling words onto the page with lyrics, melody, rhythm and rhyme; to create visual worlds where you, the reader, can live within the stories. Whether it's a narrative of a childhood memory, a funny commentary about faith from the literal son of a preacher-man, or a frolic of pure fantasy, the goal of *all* my works is to make you *feel something* by the time you reach 'THE END.'

More from Andy Bozeman

IF I'D KNOWN THAT WAS GOING TO HAPPEN WHEN I BUILT MY HOUSE, I MIGHT'VE GONE CAMPING INSTEAD

How to avoid the most common home-building mistakes.

Even More from Andy Bozeman can be found on his Amazon Author Page.
http://www.amazon.com/author/andybozeman

This Publication:
Eva's Pitcher and the Panther
Author – Andy Bozeman

ISBN 978-1-887892-08-7

www.ingramcontent.com/pod-product-compliance
Lightning Source LLC
Chambersburg PA
CBHW031142270326
41931CB00007B/662

9781887892087